Teaching Little Fingers to Play

THE BEATLES

Piano Solos with Optional Teacher Accompaniments

Arranged by
Christopher Hussey

ISBN 978-1-5400-6768-5

EXCLUSIVELY DISTRIBUTED BY

Visit Hal Leonard Online at
www.halleonard.com

Contact us:
Hal Leonard
7777 West Bluemound Road
Milwaukee, WI 53213
Email: info@halleonard.com

In Europe, contact:
Hal Leonard Europe Limited
42 Wigmore Street
Marylebone, London, W1U 2RN
Email: info@halleonardeurope.com

In Australia, contact:
Hal Leonard Australia Pty. Ltd.
4 Lentara Court
Cheltenham, Victoria, 3192 Australia
Email: info@halleonard.com.au

Who are the Beatles?

The Beatles were a four-person band from Liverpool, England that were very, very famous in the 1960s. They were known for their extremely enthusiastic fans, their fashionable hair styles, and of course, their brilliant songs. Today they are still regarded by many musicians as the most influential rock band of all time.

The members of the band were: John Lennon, Paul McCartney, George Harrison, and Ringo Starr.

CONTENTS

Hint!—
Both hands share Middle C. Pay attention to
the left hand (L.H.) movement in the last two
measures. You will need to move between the
A and G more quickly than before.

Student Position
One octave higher when performing as a duet

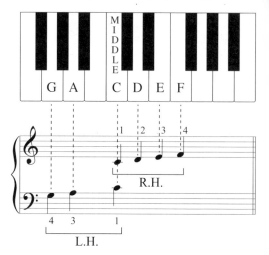

Eight Days a Week
Optional Teacher Accompaniment

Words and Music by John Lennon
and Paul McCartney
Arranged by Christopher Hussey

Joyfully, with a bounce

Eight Days a Week

Words and Music by John Lennon
and Paul McCartney
Arranged by Christopher Hussey

Play both hands one octave higher when performing as a duet.

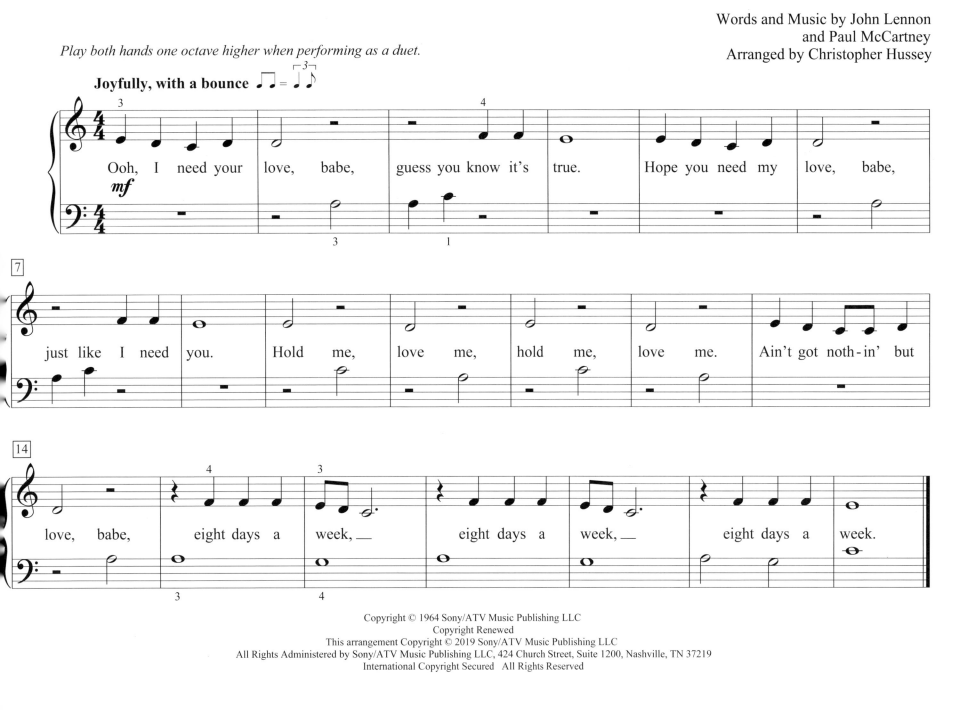

Hint!—

Enjoy the two sweeping scale-like phrases in the first half of this piece. Play them as smoothly as possible, and grow in sound as you approach the high points – the 4th-finger Fs in measures 3 and 11.

Student Position

One octave higher when performing as a duet

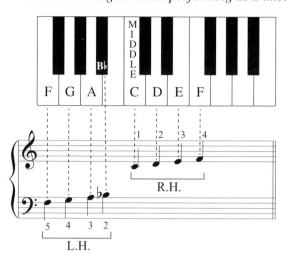

All My Loving
Optional Teacher Accompaniment

Words and Music by John Lennon
and Paul McCartney
Arranged by Christopher Hussey

All My Loving

Words and Music by John Lennon
and Paul McCartney
Arranged by Christopher Hussey

Play both hands one octave higher when performing as a duet.

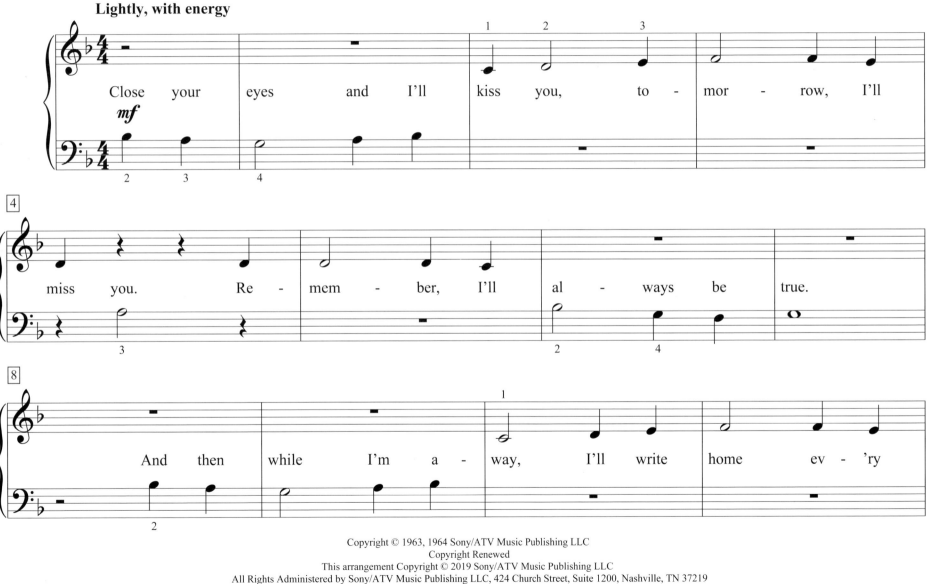

Optional Teacher Accompaniment

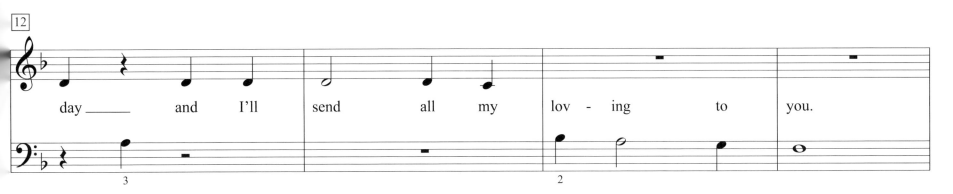

day _____ and I'll send all my lov - ing to you.

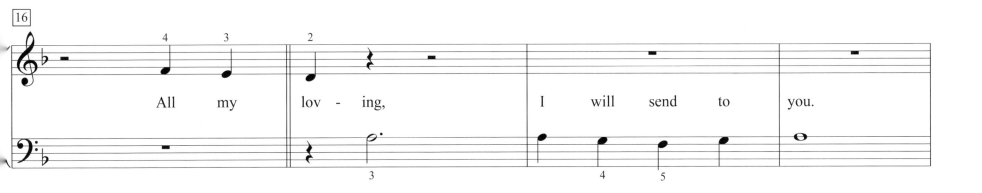

All my lov - ing, I will send to you.

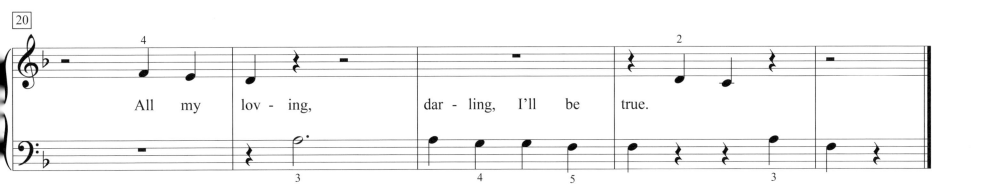

All my lov - ing, dar - ling, I'll be true.

Hint!—
Pay attention to the fingering in mm. 8 and 26, where the right hand (R.H.) 2nd finger crosses over the thumb.

Student Position
One octave higher when performing as a duet

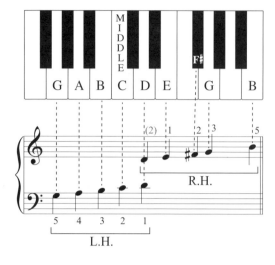

And I Love Her
Optional Teacher Accompaniment

Words and Music by John Lennon
and Paul McCartney
Arranged by Christopher Hussey

And I Love Her

Words and Music by John Lennon
and Paul McCartney
Arranged by Christopher Hussey

Play both hands one octave higher when performing as a duet.

12

Optional Teacher Accompaniment

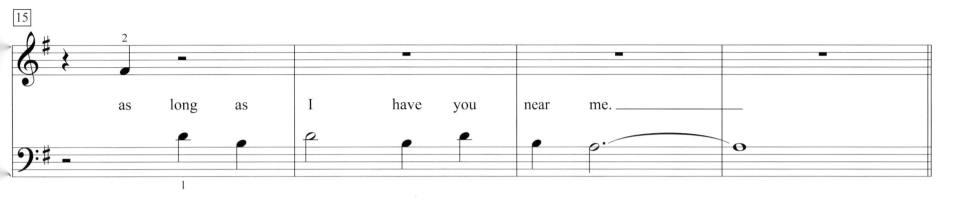

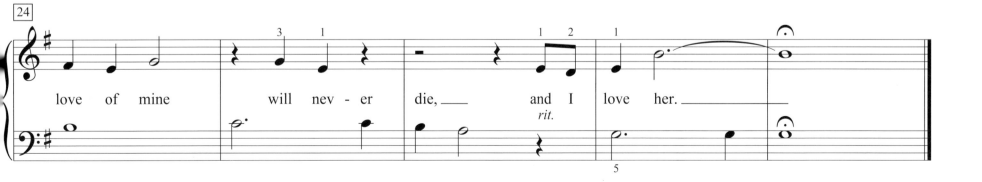

Hint!—
All five fingers are used in each hand, with
no change of position. Make the melody as
smooth as possible when changing hands
(mm. 8, 24).

Student Position
One octave higher when performing as a duet

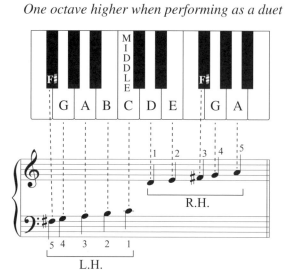

Hey Jude
Optional Teacher Accompaniment

Words and Music by John Lennon
and Paul McCartney
Arranged by Christopher Hussey

Hey Jude

Words and Music by John Lennon
and Paul McCartney
Arranged by Christopher Hussey

Play both hands one octave higher when performing as a duet.

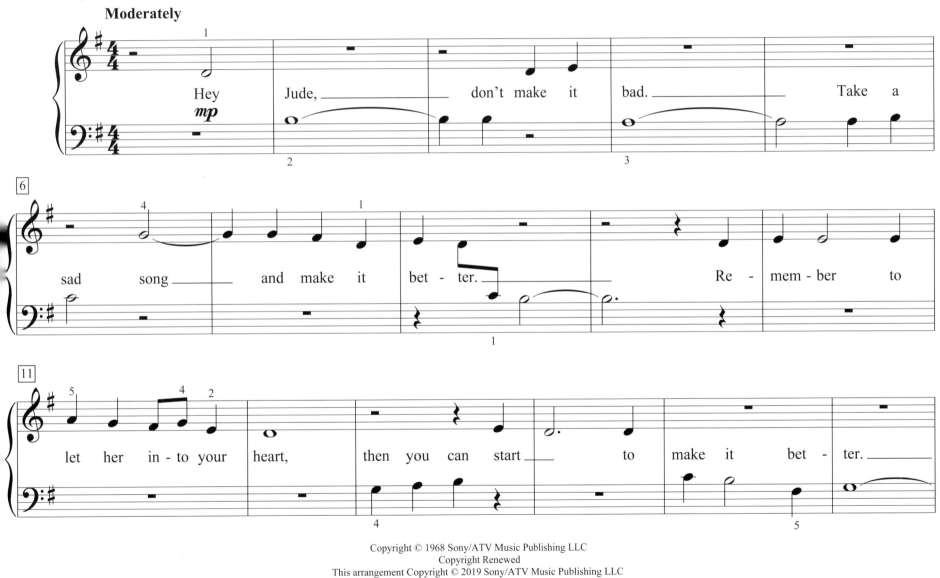

16

Optional Teacher Accompaniment

Hint!—
Pay close attention to the fingering, as well as the two R.H. positions shown in the diagram.

Student Position
One octave higher when performing as a duet

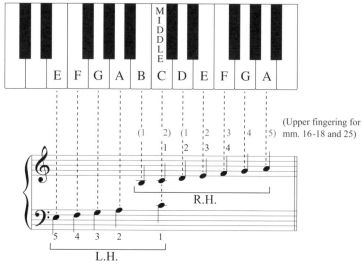

E F G A B C D E F G A

(Upper fingering for mm. 16-18 and 25)

R.H.

L.H.

Let It Be
Optional Teacher Accompaniment

Words and Music by John Lennon
and Paul McCartney
Arranged by Christopher Hussey

Solemnly

Let It Be

Words and Music by John Lennon
and Paul McCartney
Arranged by Christopher Hussey

Play both hands one octave higher when performing as a duet.

Solemnly

mp

When I find my-self in times of trou-ble, — Moth-er Mar — y comes to me, —

speak-ing — words of wis-dom, let it be. — And

in my hour of dark-ness, she is — stand-ing — right in front of me, —

Optional Teacher Accompaniment

speak-ing ___ words of wis - dom, let it be. ___ Let it ___ be, let it ___

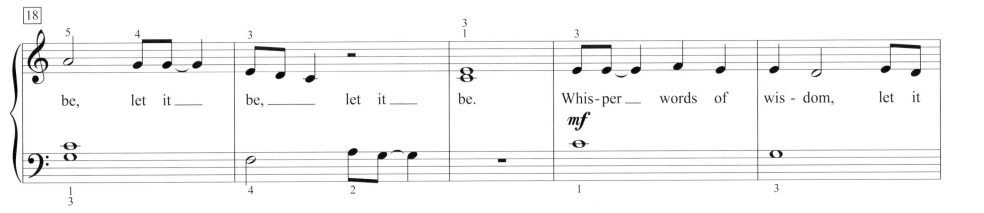

be, let it ___ be, ___ let it ___ be. Whis-per ___ words of wis - dom, let it

be. ___

22

Hint!—
Both hands share D in this piece. Be ready for a brief change in hand position in mm. 29 and 30. Watch out for the dotted rhythms in mm. 6, 7, 30 and 31, where the L.H. 4th and 5th fingers can shine.

Student Position
One octave higher when performing as a duet

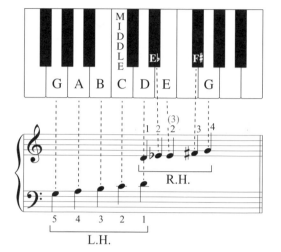

Nowhere Man
Optional Teacher Accompaniment

Words and Music by John Lennon
and Paul McCartney
Arranged by Christopher Hussey

Smoothly and thoughtfully

Nowhere Man

Words and Music by John Lennon
and Paul McCartney
Arranged by Christopher Hussey

Play both hands one octave higher when performing as a duet.

Smoothly and thoughtfully

24

Optional Teacher Accompaniment

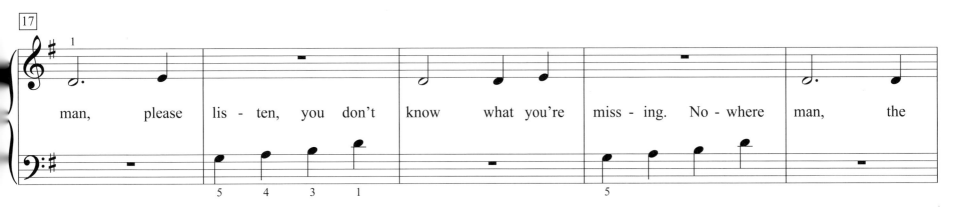

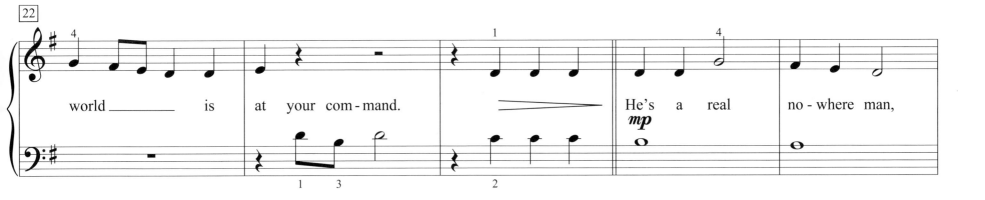

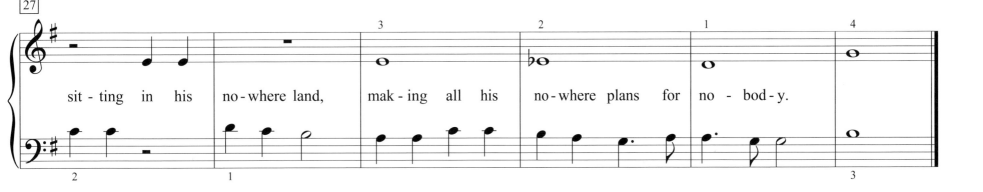

Hint!—
The left hand crosses over in mm. 5 and 14.
Put a little extra emphasis on the chord for
the word "yeah!" in m. 4.

Student Position
One octave higher when performing as a duet

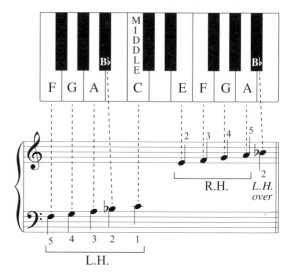

Ticket to Ride
Optional Teacher Accompaniment

Words and Music by John Lennon
and Paul McCartney
Arranged by Christopher Hussey

Ticket to Ride

Words and Music by John Lennon
and Paul McCartney
Arranged by Christopher Hussey

Play both hands one octave higher when performing as a duet.

Hint!—
Listen to the Beatles' song and you will understand what a "swing" or "swung" feel means! Make the most of the swing feel and establish a firm entry into the chorus at m. 17.

Student Position
One octave higher when performing as a duet

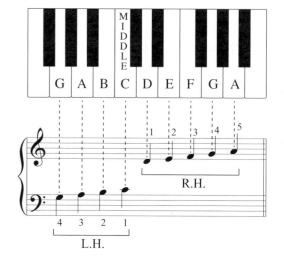

Yellow Submarine
Optional Teacher Accompaniment

Words and Music by John Lennon
and Paul McCartney
Arranged by Christopher Hussey

Yellow Submarine

Words and Music by John Lennon
and Paul McCartney
Arranged by Christopher Hussey

Play both hands one octave higher when performing as a duet.

In the town where I was born lived a man who sailed to sea. And he told us of his life in the land of sub-mar-ines. So we sailed on to the sun, 'til we found the sea of green. And we

Optional Teacher Accompaniment

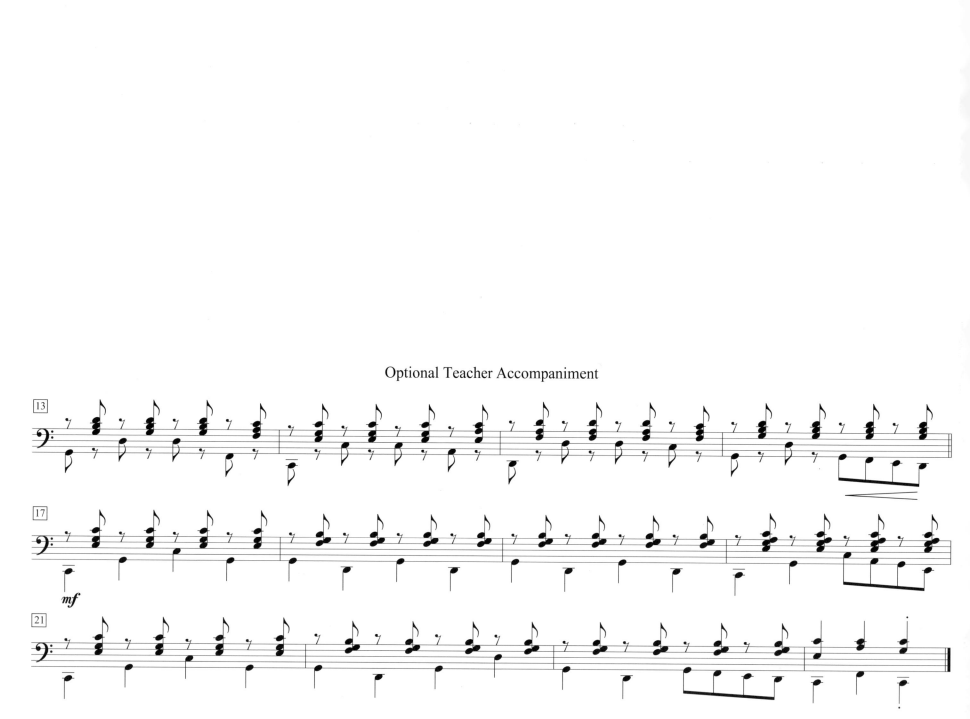

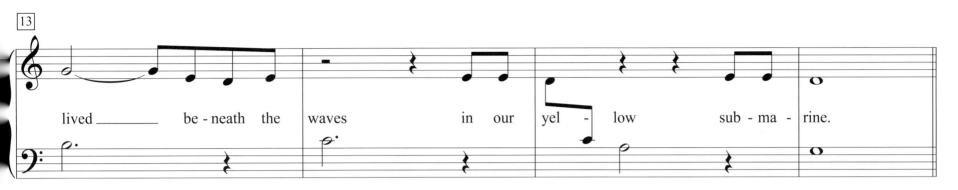

lived _____ be - neath the waves in our yel - low sub - ma - rine.

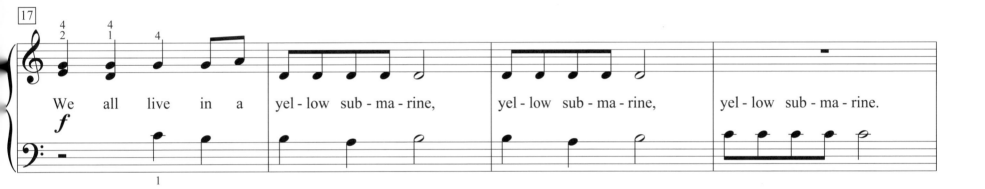

We all live in a yel - low sub - ma - rine, yel - low sub - ma - rine, yel - low sub - ma - rine.

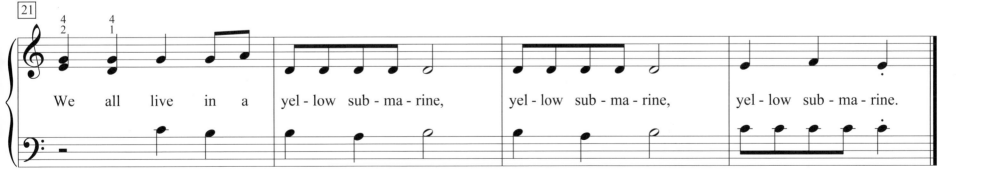

We all live in a yel - low sub - ma - rine, yel - low sub - ma - rine, yel - low sub - ma - rine.

TEACHING LITTLE FINGERS TO PLAY

TEACHING LITTLE FINGERS TO PLAY

by John Thompson

A series for the early beginner combining rote and note approach. The melodies are written with careful thought and are kept as simple as possible, yet they are refreshingly delightful. All the music lies within the grasp of the child's small hands.

00412076 Book only $7.99
00406523 Book/Audio $10.99

TEACHING LITTLE FINGERS TO PLAY ENSEMBLE

by John Thompson

A book of intermediate-level accompaniments for use in the teacher's studio or at home. Two possible accompaniments are included for each *Teaching Little Fingers* piece: a Secondo or Primo part, as well as a second piano part for studios that have two pianos/keyboards.

00412228 Book only $6.99

DISNEY TUNES

arr. Glenda Austin

10 delightful Disney songs: The Bare Necessities • Can You Feel the Love Tonight • Candle on the Water • God Help the Outcasts • Kiss the Girl • Mickey Mouse March • The Siamese Cat Song • Winnie the Pooh • You'll Be in My Heart (Pop Version) • Zip-A-Dee-Doo-Dah.

00416748 Book only $9.99
00416749 Book/Audio $12.99

CHRISTMAS CAROLS

arr. Carolyn Miller

12 piano solos: Angels We Have Heard on High • Deck the Hall • The First Noel • Hark! The Herald Angels Sing • Jingle Bells • Jolly Old Saint Nicholas • Joy to the World! • O Come, All Ye Faithful • O Come Little Children • Silent Night • Up on the Housetop • We Three Kings of Orient Are.

00406391 Book only $7.99
00406722 Book/Audio $10.99

CLASSICS

arr. Randall Hartsell

11 piano classics: Bridal Chorus (from *Lohengrin*) (Wagner) • Can-Can (from *Orpheus in the Underworld*) (Offenbach) • Country Gardens (English Folk Tune) • A Little Night Music (from *Eine kleine Nachtmusik*) (Mozart) • Lullaby (Brahms) • Ode to Joy (from Symphony No. 9) (Beethoven) • Symphony No. 5 (Second Movement) (Tchaikovsky) • and more.

00406550 Book only $7.99
00406736 Book/Audio $10.99

HYMNS

arr. Mary K. Sallee

11 hymns: Amazing Grace • Faith of Our Fathers • For the Beauty of the Earth • Holy, Holy, Holy • Jesus Loves Me • Jesus Loves the Little Children • Joyful, Joyful, We Adore Thee • Kum Bah Yah • Praise Him, All Ye Little Children • We Are Climbing Jacob's Ladder • What a Friend We Have in Jesus.

00406413 Book only $7.99
00406731 Book/Audio $10.99

TEACHING LITTLE FINGERS TO PLAY MORE

by Leigh Kaplan

Teaching Little Fingers to Play More is a fun-filled and colorfully illustrated follow-up book to *Teaching Little Fingers to Play*. This book strengthens skills learned while easing the transition into John Thompson's *Modern Course, Book One*.

00406137 Book only $6.99
00406527 Book/Audio $10.99

MORE DISNEY TUNES

arr. Glenda Austin

9 songs, including: Circle of Life • Colors of the Wind • A Dream Is a Wish Your Heart Makes • A Spoonful of Sugar • Under the Sea • A Whole New World • and more.

00416750 Book only $9.99
00416751 Book/Audio $12.99

MORE EASY DUETS

arr. Carolyn Miller

9 more fun duets arranged for 1 piano, 4 hands: A Bicycle Built for Two (Daisy Bell) • Blow the Man Down • Chopsticks • Do Your Ears Hang Low? • I've Been Working on the Railroad • The Man on the Flying Trapeze • Short'nin' Bread • Skip to My Lou • The Yellow Rose of Texas.

00416832 Book only $7.99
00416833 Book/Audio $10.99

MORE BROADWAY SONGS

arr. Carolyn Miller

10 more fantastic Broadway favorites arranged for a young performer, including: Castle on a Cloud • Climb Ev'ry Mountain • Gary, Indiana • In My Own Little Corner • It's the Hard-Knock Life • Memory • Oh, What a Beautiful Mornin' • Sunrise, Sunset • Think of Me • Where Is Love?

00416928 Book only $6.99
00416929 Book/Audio $12.99

MORE CHILDREN'S SONGS

arr. Carolyn Miller

10 songs: The Candy Man • Do-Re-Mi • I'm Popeye the Sailor Man • It's a Small World • Linus and Lucy • The Muppet Show Theme • My Favorite Things • Sesame Street Theme • Supercalifragilisticexpialidocious • Tomorrow.

00416810 Book only $7.99
00416811 Book/Audio $12.99

WILLIS MUSIC

EXCLUSIVELY DISTRIBUTED BY
HAL•LEONARD®

0820
403

All arrangements come with optional teacher accompaniments.

FOR A COMPLETE SERIES LISTING, VISIT WWW.HALLEONARD.COM